Rookie reader®

Larry Dane Brimner

Raindrops

Illustrated by **David J. Brooks**

CHILDREN'S PRESS®
A Division of Grolier Publishing
New York London Hong Kong Sydney
Danbury, Connecticut

For Debbie Wakelee and the Bakersfield Young Authors
– L. D. B.

**For my mom, who loved me so much she didn't get mad
when I doodled on the kitchen countertops**
– Love, Dave

Reading Consultant
Linda Cornwell
Learning Resource Consultant
Indiana Department of Education

**Visit Children's Press® on the Internet at:
http://publishing.grolier.com**

Library of Congress Cataloging-in-Publication Data
Brimner, Larry Dane.
    Raindrops / by Larry Dane Brimner ; illustrated by David J. Brooks.
      p. cm. — (A rookie reader)
    Summary: Follows the water cycle, as a raindrop moves into a creek,
into a stream, into a river, and to its end in a lazy ocean.
    ISBN 0-516-21203-6 (lib.bdg.)   0-516-26477-X (pbk.)
    1. Water—Juvenile literature. [1. Hydrologic cycle. 2. Water.]
I. Brooks, David J., ill. II. Title. III. Series.
GB662.3.B75 1999
551.48—dc21   98-19036
                                       CIP
                                       AC

GROLIER
PUBLISHING

Drip! Splish! Splash! Raindrops.

First one.

4

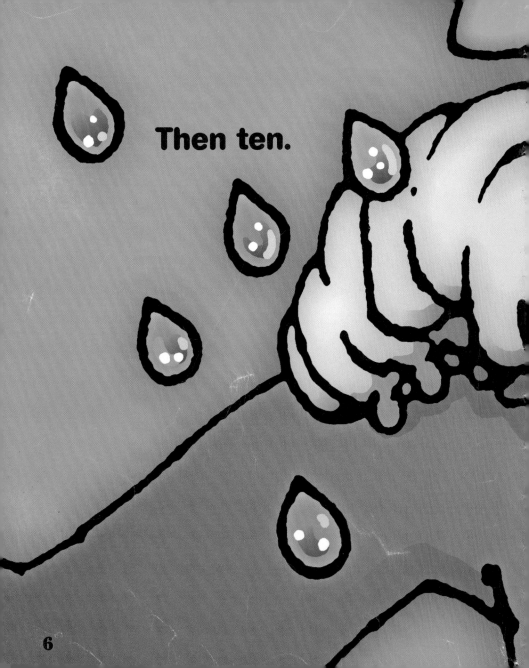

Then ten.

Then ten times ten.

11

In far-away
mountains.

Through forest leaves.

Into a rocky creek.

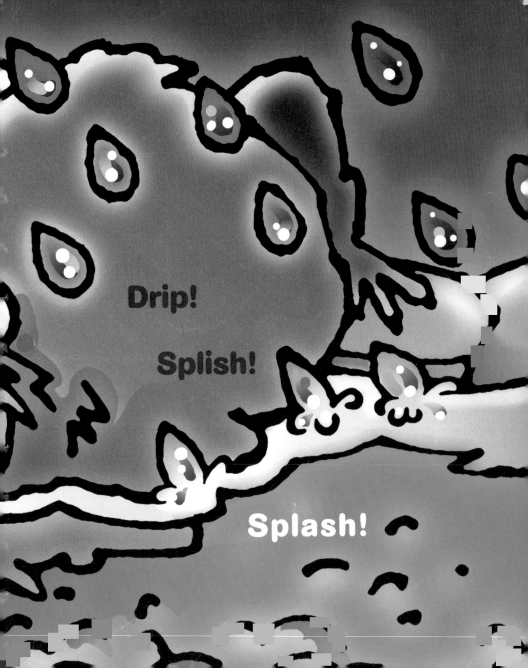

Creek joins stream.

19

Stream
joins river.

River rolls.

22

23

And roars.

24

And races.

Down canyons and into valleys...

...until it roars no more

and is lazy.

Then
under a warm
summer sun,

we sail our boat to the sea.

Word List (48 words)

a	in	races	sun
and	into	raindrops	ten
away	is	river	the
boat	it	roars	then
canyons	joins	rocky	through
creek	lazy	rolls	times
down	leaves	sail	to
drip	more	sea	under
fall	mountains	splash	until
far	no	splish	valleys
first	one	stream	warm
forest	our	summer	we

About the Author

Larry Dane Brimner writes on a wide range of topics, from picture book and middle-grade fiction to young adult nonfiction. He has written many Rookie Readers, including *Lightning Liz, Dinosaurs Dance, Aggie and Will, Nana's Hog,* and *Cowboy Up!* He lives in the southwest region of the United States.

About the Illustrator

David J. Brooks grew up in Pennsylvania, and then moved to Maine and studied art at the University of Maine. He has been a designer and illustrator in Maine for more than twenty years. David now lives in southern California where it almost never rains.